A FIRST LOOK AT FLOWERS

By Millicent E. Selsam
and Joyce Hunt

ILLUSTRATED BY HARRIETT SPRINGER

WALKER AND COMPANY ✹ NEW YORK

First published in the United States of America
in 1976 by the Walker Publishing Company, Inc.

Published simultaneously in Canada by Fitzhenry &
Whiteside, Limited, Toronto.

Trade ISBN: 0-8027-6281-6
Reinf. ISBN: 0-8027-6282-4
Library of Congress Catalog Card Number: 76-57063

Printed in the United States of America.

10 9 8 7 6 5 4 3 2 1

The authors wish to thank Dr. Howard S. Irwin, President of the New York Botanical Gardens, for checking the text of this book.

A *FIRST LOOK AT* SERIES

Each of the nature books for this series is planned to develop the child's powers of observation and give him or her a rudimentary grasp of scientific classification.

What is a flower?
A flower is part of a plant.
Here are some plants with flowers.

ROSE

MAPLE

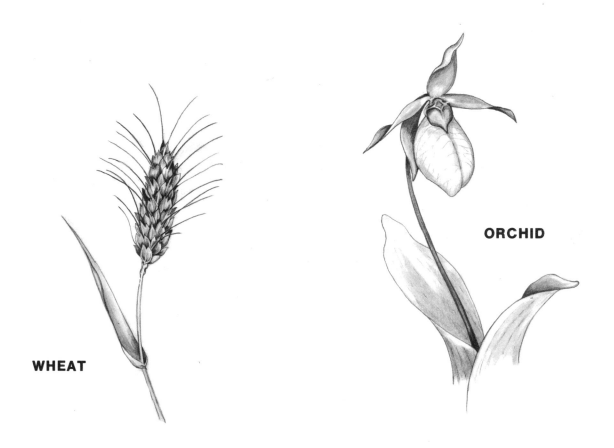

WHEAT

ORCHID

The flowers look different.
How do you tell one flower from another?

Sometimes you can tell flowers apart by their shapes.

Find the flower that looks like a bell.
Find the flower that looks like a star.
Find the flower that looks like a torch.
Find the flower that looks like a trumpet.

These three flowers are shaped like their names.
Match the flower to its name.

TURTLEHEAD

DUTCHMAN'S PIPE

DUTCHMAN'S BREECHES

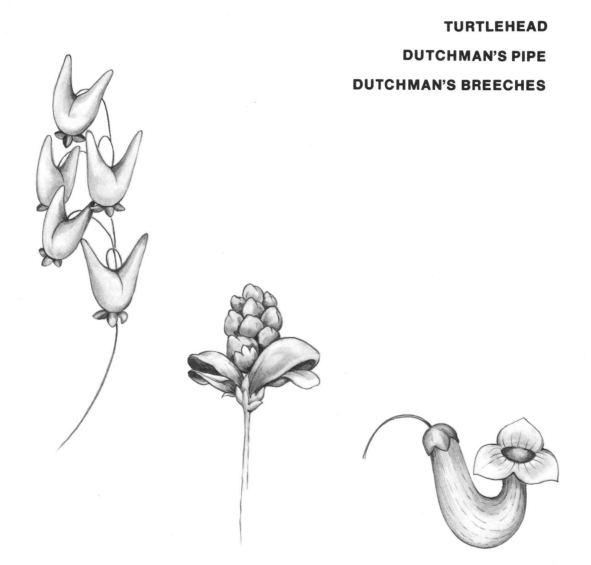

9

There are other things to look for.
Look for the way the flowers are arranged on the stalk.
Sometimes one single flower grows on a stalk.
Poppies grow this way.

But many flowers grow in groups called clusters.

Lily of the valley flowers
are arranged this way.

The little tiny flowers
of Queen Anne's Lace
grow in the shape of an umbrella.

The flowers of the gladiola
sit right on the stalk.

Here is a poppy, a lily of the valley, a
Queen Anne's Lace and a gladiola.
Which is which?

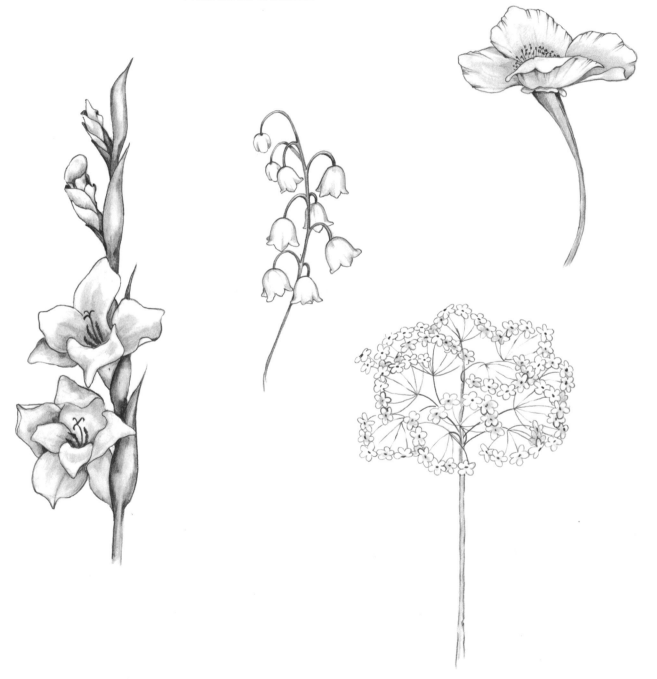

Now let us look at flowers close up.

All the petals on one flower may be
the same size and shape.

They may be separate from each other. (You can pull
each petal off without tearing any others.)

SPRING BEAUTY

—or they may be joined together.

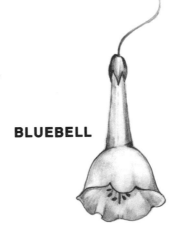

BLUEBELL

But often petals have different sizes and shapes
in the same flower.

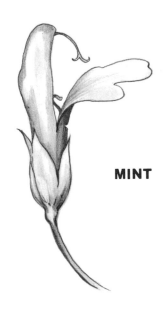

MINT

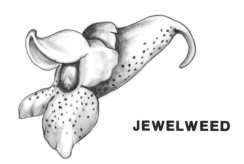

JEWELWEED

Which flower has the bottom petals ending in a spur?

Which flower looks as though it has two lips?

13

You can also tell flowers apart
by the number of their petals.

WILD HYACINTH

SPIDERWORT

EVENING PRIMROSE

VIOLET

How many petals does the evening primrose have?
The wild hyacinth?
The spiderwort?
The violet?

Here are other clues to look for.

Look for the flower with petals
that have smooth edges.
Look for the flower with petals
that look like the letter "Y."
Look for the flower with fringed petals.

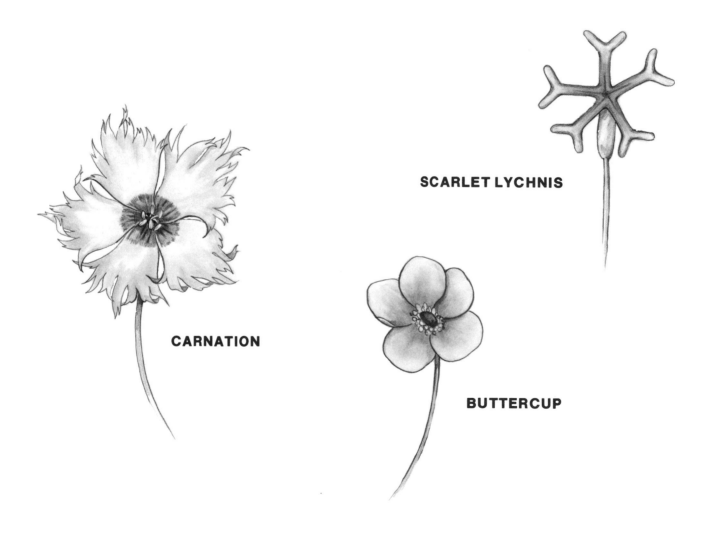

SCARLET LYCHNIS

CARNATION

BUTTERCUP

Look inside the flower to find the most important parts.

The parts that hold the pollen are called stamens.
In the rose they are hard to count because there are so many.

SMOOTH ROSE

But count the stamens in the lily and in the wild geranium.
Which has six and which has ten stamens?

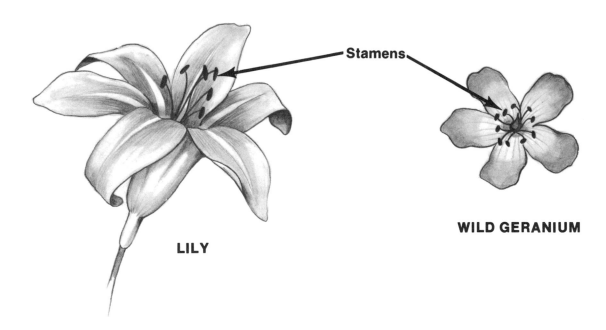

LILY

WILD GERANIUM

Stamens are sometimes joined together.

Sweet peas have ten stamens.

How many are joined together?

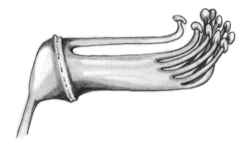

PETALS REMOVED

At the very center of the flower
is the part that makes seeds.
It is called the pistil.
The pistil can have many different shapes.

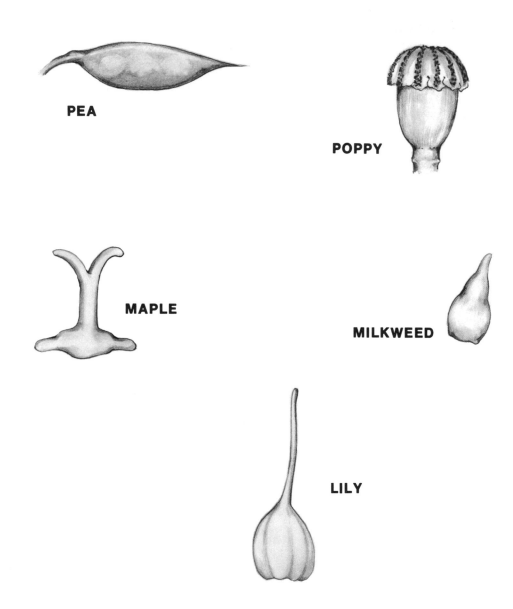

PEA

POPPY

MAPLE

MILKWEED

LILY

There can be one or more pistils in one flower.

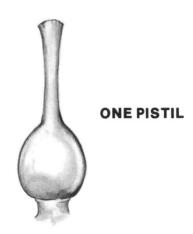

ONE PISTIL

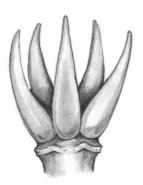

FIVE PISTILS

The pistils and the stamens can even be
in separate flowers.
For example, the oak tree has two different kinds of flowers
on the same branch.

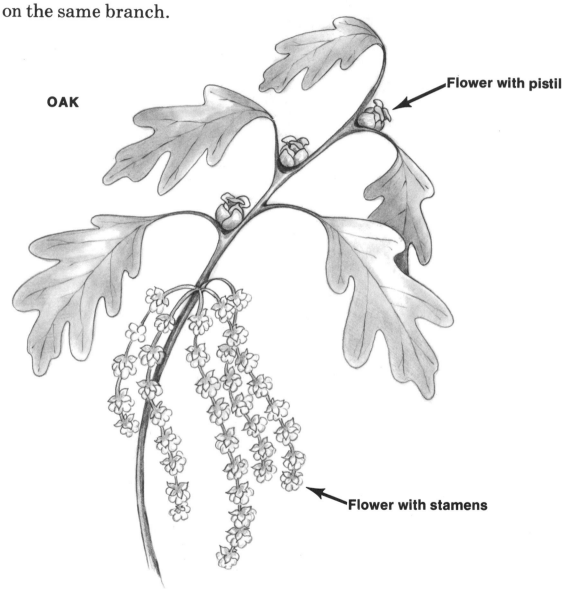

OAK

Flower with pistil

Flower with stamens

A flower is a flower if it has stamens or pistils.

Is this a flower?
It looks like one, but it really is lots of
very small flowers growing together on a head.

DANDELION HEAD

Each tiny flower has one petal
and its own stamens and pistil.

SINGLE DANDELION FLOWER

All the many things you looked for in this book
help to tell one family of flowers from another.

For example, all the flowers in the lily family
have six stamens and one pistil.

A PUZZLE:
Here are six flowers.
Five of them belong to the lily family.
Can you find the one that does not?

WILD GARLIC

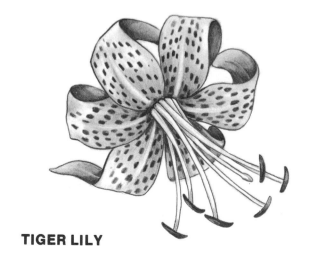

TIGER LILY

RED TRILLIUM

WILD GERANIUM

TULIP

WILD HYACINTH

How many stamens does the wild geranium have?
Does it belong to a different plant family?

Suppose you know a plant is a lily, but another lily plant
has flowers that look almost exactly like it.
Is there any other way to tell them apart?

Look at the leaves.

TURK'S CAP LILY

TIGER LILY

Now you can tell a Turk's Cap Lily from a Tiger Lily.

When you look at a flower you have to notice many things.

Look at the shape.

Look at the way the flowers are arranged on the stalk.

See if the petals are separate or joined together.

See if the petals have different sizes and shapes.

Look at the edge of the petals.

Count the petals.

Count the stamens.

Count the pistils.

Notice the shape of the pistil or pistils.

  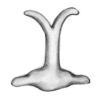

Look to see if the stamens and pistils
are in the same flower.

Look at the whole plant for other clues.

As you can see, color was not one of the ways used
to tell flowers apart. Color can be tricky.
There are white bluebells and yellow violets.
To tell a bluebell or a violet from other flowers
we must look at the parts of the flower.

How many of these flowers do you recognize?